READING POWER

Sports Training

Soccer

Jack Otten

The Rosen Publishing Group's
PowerKids Press™
New York

Published in 2002 by The Rosen Publishing Group, Inc.
29 East 21st Street, New York, NY 10010

First Edition

Book Design: Laura Stein

Photo Credits: Cover, pp. 4, 6–21 by Richard Sheinwald;
p. 5 © AFP/Corbis

Thanks to Mike Goodrich, Margo Miller, and the Coral Springs Storm soccer team

Otten, Jack.
Soccer / by Jack Otten.
    p. cm. — (Sports training)
Includes bibliographical references (p.   ) and index.
ISBN 0-8239-5972-4 (lib. bdg.)
1. Soccer—Training—Juvenile literature.   [1. Soccer.]
I. Title. II. Series: Otten, Jack. Sports training.
GV943.9.T7O88 2001
796.334'2—dc21
                                        2001001554

Manufactured in the United States of America

Contents

Introduction

This is Mia Hamm. She is a pro soccer player. Mia Hamm scores a lot of goals. These young players want to play pro soccer some day.

Warming Up

The Tigers meet for practice.
The coach tells the team to warm up.

The players stretch their legs.
Stretching loosens their muscles.

The players also run around the field to warm up. Running builds strong legs. Strong legs help soccer players run fast and kick hard.

Strong Legs

This player practices charging the ball. Charging the ball helps players block passes.

Blocking a Pass

Soccer players wear spiked shoes. Spiked shoes help players turn and stop fast.

Spiked Shoe

Learning Skills

The coach shows each player how to pass the ball. Players must pass the ball to each other.

The coach passes the ball to a player. The player stops the pass with her foot. She does not touch the ball with her hands.

The coach kicks a high pass. The player blocks the high pass with her body.

The player moves the ball as she runs. She kicks the ball with the inside part of her foot.

The player runs at the ball. She is going to kick the ball hard.

The goalie stands in front of the goal. She wears gloves to keep her hands safe.

Goal

Gloves

She reaches out with her hands. She blocks the ball from going into the goal.

Block

A Practice Game

The Tigers play a practice game.
They pass and kick the ball the way
the coach has taught them.

The coach tells the team that they practiced well.

"Great practice, team!"

Glossary

goal (**gohl**) a large box with a net into which soccer players try to kick the ball

goalie (**goh**-lee) a soccer player who stops balls from going into the goal

pass (**pas**) when a player kicks the soccer ball to another player on his or her team

practice (**prak**-tihs) to do something again and again

spiked shoes (**spykt shooz**) shoes that have sharp points on the bottom to help players move or stop quickly

warm up (**worm uhp**) to get the body ready to play a sport

Resources

Books
Soccer
by Laurie Wark
Kids Can Press (1994)

Starting Soccer
by Helen Edom
Usborne Publishing Ltd. (1999)

Web Site
All About Soccer
http://members.aol.com/msdaizy/sports/soccer.html

Index

Word Count: 249

Note to Librarians, Teachers, and Parents

If reading is a challenge, Reading Power is a solution! Reading Power is perfect for readers who want high-interest subject matter at an accessible reading level. These fact-filled, photo-illustrated books are designed for readers who want straightforward vocabulary, engaging topics, and a manageable reading experience. With clear picture/text correspondence, leveled Reading Power books put the reader in charge. Now readers have the power to get the information they want and the skills they need in a user-friendly format.